I Am A Freedom Writer

A BOOK OF THOUGHTS, POEMS & SHORT STORIES

Brandon Mackey

Copyright © 2021 by Brandon Mackey

All rights reserved.

No part of this book may be reproduced in any form or by any electronic or mechanical means, including information storage and retrieval systems, without permission from the author, except for the use of brief quotation in a book review.

This book is dedicated to my mom. Without her I wouldn't be who I am today. She made a way for me out of no way. She took me and my siblings away from a town that had gang violence and crime and placed us in a city that moved at a slower pace, but kept me from going down a dark road. All my greatness comes from you, MOM. I love you so much.

Out of My Soul

I see myself on the ground wearing a hoodie with jeans and blood all around. While I lay on the ground I see the bad people talking so they can cover up the truth with a lie and I'm asking myself why can't they tell the truth. They didn't fear me because if they did they wouldn't be laughing out loud. They would be crying out loud and going crazy and asking "what do we do now?", instead they were so chill about it and that ain't right. I feel my soul getting cold as I watch my body slow down, while my blood keeps leaking on the ground. Then a news crew comes on the scene and asks what happened and the bad people tell their lies to cover up the truth and paint a bad picture of me so I know as long as I'm out of my soul before my body gets too cold. I must get to the bottom of this and make the news people feel the truth so I can set my soul free so my body can rest in peace.

Black Queen

Black Queen I hear you and I see you.
I fear for your life.
One day I will make you my wife.
You were the only one who helped birth the nation, cook, and clean for people who hated you with a passion and made sure us black men were ok after we went through some action after you've been working all day without relaxing.
Black Queen you must keep pushing and get that dirt up off of your shoulders.
Black Queen if they ever truly wanted to stop our culture all they have to do is stop you and we would be truly lost.
Black Queen, you are the most undervalued and disrespected human in this nation.
Black Queen I feel your pain from all of the hate that comes after you all because they don't see or hear you .
Keep moving forward and making them fear you because you are the truth and you are beautiful.
Black Queen and I will forever love you.

A Text 2 My Haters

Curiosity killed the cat but a snitch birthed a rat.
So if you are a coward or a chicken please stay the fuck back.
I got a monkey on my shoulder and I aint taking no crap.
I see snakes in the grass.
Keep fucking with me and that will be your ass.
Keep playing possum if you want to and watch me run your ass over.
I'm the goat because I give everybody in my city hope.
I barely made it through this year, 2020 it's been a hell of a year.
I do not want to hear any of your bullshit you were trying to tell me.
Just to let you know if the beaver sees his shadow yall going to be in trouble.
I heard it was the year of the dog.
I guess it's time for me to be what some of you females claim me to be and I guess that means some of you female's are female dogs and it is a dog on shame that I had to say that.
Some of yall act like yall got that skunk, but all you are smoking is roaches that someone left behind some of yall are faker than some of your animal school mascots.
They say I'm bananas for writing this, I say fuck it, let's go ham cuz I don't give a damn.
I'll do it again because this is a text, to my haters.

White Hate Is Real

Why do you hate us so much?
Is it because our skin is the same color as God?
If so, let me know.
Is it because we can stay in and soak in the sun without burning?
Is that it or is it because we were your pets and you treated us worse than dog shit and now we are the shit and not your pets anymore?
If so, please let that go because we will not be going back to that ever and that's a promise or is it because we are kings and queens and we can be anything we want if we truly believe?
Or is it because we were last but now we are first or is it because everything we do y'all steal?
Is it so yall can say y'all did it first because we are the original trendsettaz?
Why do you hate us so much but love and try your best to live in our culture?
Please make me understand that part because we aren't dumb like you make us out to be and why didn't you want us to read or write back in the day?
Why did you feed our babies to the creatures in the swamps if you didn't hate us so much?
So, since now you have read this and said you don't hate us and that is a damn lie and let me be real, I need to stop saying yall putting all white people in the same category because some of yall really love the color black and brown that is on our skin and it's only a few of yall and we love you all and y'all are welcome to the BBQ and to the other half that is yelling make america great again, fuck you all and your leader beacause the hate you have for us is not welcomed at all.
I want to end this by saying white is not fake white hate is real.

Black Caucasian

You are black as black can be when it comes to your skin color, but you hate your sisters and brothers of the same color because you think you are another color. All because you think white is the superior color you try your very best to make sure the color black ain't blessed. You are almost worse than a Karen because a Karen is your new best friend you love his stories but hate people of color history you been brainwashed for so long that being black to you is dead wrong when you are around a lot of black people you feel all alone but when you are around a lot of white people and you are the only person of color you feel at home and not alone at all. You hate your hair because it is black, you hate your skin because it is black. If you had the power to change it you would in a heartbeat to any color but black all because you don't think black lives matter at all. You just wish all black lives would take a fall and never get back up at all. All because you are a black caucasian.

Time is the Love of My Life

She told me once she leaves that I will never get her back. I told her to give me a second to think about it, please. She said NO! But as she was going away I dropped to my knees and said wait a minute please. She said OK. Let me hear what you got to say. I said "Why are you going to do me like that?" She says "You better count your blessings that I'm still here and I stay the same every year, but you change. Why did you change?" I replied " Because of you." She says "That's a damn lie." I reply "No, it's the cold hearted truth." Then she asks me "Why iam always talking about killing her everytime I do something I don't like or don't want to do?" I say "I don't know why I do that, I can't help it." Then she says " The only time you notice me is when I'm clocking in or getting off of work and I only love her during daylight saving time. I tell her " That's not true." But she still says I'm a damn liar. She said I know who she is because I live by her. I track my life with her and that I can't live without her. I told her that is true, that's why I want to marry you. Then I said you are all I got and you are the love of my life. I'm so sorry I took you for granted and I promise to this day forward before I leave this planet I won't do it again. Then I said will you be mine forever?" She said yes, so I got up off my knees and realized that I am blessed to have her on my side in my life, that's why I made her my wife. Because time is the love of my life.

Too Many Late Nites

At the age of 16 she is going out to the nightclubs trying to be grown but she is only in the 9th grade and she doesn't see anything wrong with that. She is telling guys lies that she got her own home but she lives at home with her folks. She tells her mom she is having a sleepover at a friend's house every weekend. She has a fake ID, plus her driving license and she loves getting paid at a young age. One night a guy paid her for sex and left her without telling her he had AIDS. Over time she got really sick and skinny. She used to be super thick, but now she is very sick and fighting for her life all because she had one night too many.

What is Black History?

Black is everything to me. It is more than skin deep. It is 400 years plus of slaving for the white master. It is loving our God more than we love our pastor. They didn't want us to learn how to read or write back then, so it's about dying for our knowledge. It's knowing about Black Wall St. and what they did to us because they are the dangerous ones, not us. It is catching a bus and being forced to sit in the back. It is seeing WHITE ONLY signs and having fear of going near it. It is getting killed because of your darker skin because we were told black is bad and white is good. It is our black females helping with everything just to be told that they are not shit. It is Malcolm and Martin coming together for our future. It is about a white man saying "Don't move nigger, before I shoot you." It is being guilty because of the color of your skin. It is our beautiful babies getting fed to creatures in the swamp. It is Brianna Taylor never waking up from her beauty sleep. It is George Floyd saying " I can't breathe." and getting put to permanent sleep on national tv so that the world can see his killers still walk free. It is Emmett Till getting killed and never getting to live his life or meet his wife. It is our black musicians getting robbed of their music from the industry and the industry saying they sold their soul. It is about blacks getting treated less than dog shit. It is about being told a lie is the truth and the truth is a flat out lie. It is being called a dummy after they made sure we don't learn how to read or write. It is about marching for our rights and that is what our history is like. Just a tiny bit of what black history is really like.

Let the Old Man Talk

You're saying I'm blessed because I'm 90 plus in years. I hear what you are saying but you don't feel my pain and when I fall I can't get back up. I feel stuck because if you did feel my pain, it would drive you insane and you would be like what the fuck. The love of my life is gone and my kids put me in a home and they are gone, but they are not dead but they don't come see me at all. I'm all alone and I don't have a place to call home. I hear what you are trying to say, but do you hear me while I'm in here in your face? I am the guy who used to be 6 ft but now I'm 5 ft and weak. In this place I'm staying, the people are so mean to me. I fear them, they make me keep my bed wet and they are always picking on me and I'm a vet. I thought they're supposed to show so much respect to me because of that. I hate veteran's day with a passion because that's the day I get so much fake love. They are nice to me on that day only and they want to take pictures with me and put it on their little phone tv and when they have a problem at home they come to work and take it out on me. If their husbands, boyfriend, or side dude beat on them, then they beat on me and call me by their name so that they don't feel shame for beating me. So, do you still think I'm blessed? If so, I'll let you keep thinking that but I had to give you a reality check.

Hey Karen

A black guy is on his phone. "Hey, Karen!!!" put down your phone. A black family is enjoying family time at home. "Hey, Karen!!!" put down your phone. A black baby is crying. "Hey, Karen!!!" put down your phone. Why are you on your phone? A black kid is selling lemonade so he can get paid. "Hey, Karen!!!" Why are you so afraid? What's wrong and don't even think about getting your phone. A black kid is walking to school. "Hey, Karen!!!" What's with the phone that ain't cool and you are looking like a fool. A black woman is selling real estate. "Hey, Karen!!!" Get off your damn phone. Why must you hate? A black couple who are first time home buyers celebrating? "Hey, Karen!!!" I see you over there with two phones still hating. A black person is talking about politics. "Hey, Karen!!!" Why are you messing with your damn phone, leave him alone. You know what Karen, you make me so damn sick of you and that's the damn truth. A black man is trying to buy land. "Hey, Karen!!!" I don't understand why you got both of your phones out. Just let the man buy his land in peace so he can build his home so that his family can have a place to call home. Whoever answers the phone on the other end when Karen makes her favorite call, yall know that you are so damn wrong and fuck you all especially Karen and her phones.

Two Different Prayer Request

Jerome and Donald are praying to the same GOD. Jerome's prayer requests never get answered, but Donald's prayer requests get answered every time. Jerome is a good man. He's never been in trouble with the law a day in his life and he loves his kids and his wife. He lives paycheck to paycheck and barely has any money to save his neck, while Donald is filthy rich and never worked a day in his life. He cheats and beats on his wife. He steals from the poor with his business. He never ever paid his taxes a day in his life and he is a pastor of a megachurch. Jerome gets discriminated against because of his race, while Donald gets high praises when he walks into any place. Jerome has more faith than anybody in this world, while Donald has no faith in GOD and tries his best to be GOD of this world. You can't tell Donald anything because he thinks he knows everything, while Jerome listens and pays close attention because he wants to learn something. Jerome is always praying for his family and friends, while Donald is always praying for something with a sin. Let that sink in.

10 Four

Roger was in the army to be all that he can be, but when he got set free, back to regular life, he lost his mind. He wasn't used to that life after 15 years in the army and 3 tours. He felt like less than a man with a purple heart. The army forgot all about him. All he knew was the army and war but that is no more so he drank and smoked his pain away, chasing a new high on a day to day. He didn't have kids or a wife and that's why he hated life. Everything he did after the army he couldn't get it right at all. When he got home after 15 years everyone he loved was in jail, heaven, or hell. He felt so alone and killing himself was on his mind daily but God wouldn't let him die because it wasn't his time to fly high so he would get high and let the time pass him by waiting for the day he can die and see everyone he once loved up in heaven up above. His childhood friend, a girl, came into his life and made everything alright so he made her his wife and this is the story of Roger's life. Do you copy that? 10 four over and out.

Young King

A young boy named King was born on June 19th after his parents were set free for years. King knew he was special because his mom told him so. But he didn't know why so late at night he would sit up in the bed and ask God "Why?" then he would cry himself to sleep. King is living in a time on Earth where the color of your skin can get you killed but King didn't know why and when King would walk around town with his dad he would see a lot of "White Only" signs.

He didn't know what they meant because he couldn't read so he remembered the words in his head and was set on finding out what they meant because they were everywhere they went. His dad worked in a mill and his mom cleaned houses so he could have a place to chill. He noticed his dad would always act like the white man in front of the white man but he never knew why.

As years went by King got older and smarter. He loved working out and drinking water. Before his dad passed away, King remembered what he said to him one day "Black is King" and it stuck with King throughout his life. His dad died from stress because he tried his very best to please the white man with his work but it was never good enough until his dad took his permanent rest and King let that weight rest on his chest for years wondering why his dad wasn't good enough for the white man. When it came to being a worker for the white man, his dad was the very best and there was nobody better.

When his dad died it took 10 people plus 3 machines to do his job at work. At that point in his life King had so much hate in his heart for the white man, you could see it in his face but his mom made him realize he couldn't make a change with hate in his heart but he could make a change with his smarts. At that time in his life people with his skin color didn't have the right to vote. King never understood back then why the white man hated black skin so much.

Other World

I want to live in a world where Treyvon can wear a hoodie and drink his tea with some skittles of his choice. I want to be a part of the world where Mr. Aubrey could break a sweat running and not die. I want to see a world where Breonna Taylor wakes up after her beautiful night of sleep. I wish I could see a world where George could breathe forever. I need to see a world where Mr. Mackey was set free from jail. I want to see a world where Michael Brown has grown up and changed his life and found his wife.

I want to see a world where Castille is teaching kids the importance of a good education and having a carry permit and taking his wife and kid on a vacation. I want to be on a planet where Eric Garner can sell or smoke a cigarette in peace. I want to be on an Earth where Emmett Till didn't have to die because of a lie. I wish I could see a world where Sandra was still alive with us after a traffic stop all because of some crooked cops. I wish I was in a world where Martin could tell me more about his dreams. I want to be in a world where babies of color weren't fed to creatures in a swamp. I want to be in a world where Black Wall St. is still around and Rosewood didn't get burnt down.

I want to hear of a world where black soldiers who fought for America who didn't come back from war just to be jailed or killed. I want to live in a world where there is liberty and justice for all. I want to see a world where you can get the same time for the same crime no matter your color. I want to see a world where Tamir Rice can play with a toy gun as a kid just for fun and grow up to have a future. I want to see a world where Alton Sterling was still with us and becoming a music producer if he wanted to. I want to be a part of a world where black people are treated equally and free from white hate.

I want to see a world where Mrs. Jefferson was safe at her own home with her windows up and letting fresh air in her home and she wasn't alone. I want to be a part of a world where Stephon Clark was still here with us after having his phone. I want to see a world where Botham Jean can chill in his own home and relax. I want to see a world where Freddie Gray was still here after being in a police van. I wish I could see a world where Akai Gurley didn't have to die because of an evil cop and this must stop. Will I ever get to see this other world before I die?

Can You Tell Me Why?

Can you tell me the truth and not a lie? Can you tell me who I am so I know before I die? Can you tell me why our life doesn't matter and yalls do? Can you tell me what's wrong with my skin color so I won't get killed by a bad cop? Can you tell me why our life is harder than most? Can you tell me why our life can't get right and why yall keep trying to take away our rights? Can you tell me why we can't take a knee when the flag song comes on, when people fought for us to have the freedom to do so? Can you tell me why our lives don't matter to the court system at all? Please tell me why black lives don't matter in yall eyes at all because we don't deserve to die not at all.

The Walls are Finally Talking

The walls are telling it all. People are losing their minds trying to hide their soul while the walls are talking and getting bold with it. Got a pastor who left church because of what the walls said to him. Really hurt him. Got a cop who arrested himself because the walls said he needed some help. Got a female who got sick because the walls called her a bitch. I saw a CEO of a big building cry because the walls told him he's not going to live forever and he's going to die. I saw a big man fall to his knees and begged the walls, please, not to tell his wife on him. I saw a judge give himself 25 to life all because the walls said he must judge right all because the walls are not playing at all in the day or night. They will not stop talking. The walls will make your worst fears hurt you and the walls can't lie because all they know is the truth.

Let Me Draw You

I see the circle that started you. I see the line that created you . I see the shade that helped you to be you and without color you are so beautiful, but with color you are more beautiful than the eyes can hold. You don't need a background to stand out. You don't need anything to be erased because that would be a big mistake and a disgrace cause I like you just the way you are. Your beauty is art, that's why you have my heart. The color of your eyes are diamonds in disguise. I see the detail in your soul. It looks so beautiful and bold and it looks like heaven and not hell. I see the wild in you, it makes me want to yell for joy because I am so happy to be with you. All I ask of you, is that you let my heart continue to draw you closer to me so that I can love you for eternity while your colors of love run forever deep into my heart and leak into my soul.

The Real Is

The real gang members wear blue and say blue lives matter and the real drug dealers will see you in the E.R. or if you make an appointment you can come to their offices. If you ever want to meet the real mob boss just get in trouble with the law and get a court date and the boss will be right in your face on that date. The real junkies are the low class people who they really don't see because they think less of them. But if you let them tell it then it would be the other way around and put it all on the low class people all because they are so damn evil. They think we are worthless all because they are fake sensitive and it's a damn shame they got the world believing the lie.

She is a Dead Beat

She is always talking to random guys from the internet and she has two kids that she doesn't want to see. Even Though they want to see her so badly, she always says she doesn't have time but she will make time for new guys from the internet anytime and will waste all of her dimes on them and will not spend a penny on her kids, what a damn shame. All because she wants attention from a damn man. She doesn't have a game plan for life. All she knows is one day she might be someone's wife but she doesn't care. Her baby dad keeps telling her how great the kids are doing so she acts fake and says "tell them mommy loves them" but never ever gives them hugs and kisses for them to feel love from a mother. She will be a mother to another guy's kids just to make that guy happy, what a damn shame. She is what you call a dead beat.

The Pain in His Eyes

He ain't no pimp. He is just a junkie. He pimps out his girlfriend so that he can get a fix and when he gets mad at her he calls her a bitch. He never found real love, so he settles for drugs day in and day out. Before he shoots up, he would cry his pain away and then put his lighter to his face as he puts the needle in the right place. Then he falls asleep and wishes his pain would fade away like yesterday. When he awakes, you should see the look on his face. He is so mad that he is still here on Earth because everyone who really loved him, has already left this Earth. Every night he hopes to go to sleep and see their faces in another place, but it never happens so he just drinks and shoots up his pain, wishing his life would fade away just like yesterday. All he wants is a better way, he just doesn't know how that's why you see the pain in his eyes.

Plz Don't Forget Me

Please remember me as I was and not as I am. Please don't forget me because I can't lose you while you're alive, it will hurt deep down inside. Please look at me with your eyes so maybe it can bring back a vision and it can be a surprise. Please feel my skin, maybe it will make you realize that we are kin. Please remember and don't forget me again plz because I need you. Because you are my best friend. Please hold my hand while we dance in your memories because all I want to do is set your memories free. Just know that if you can't remember me it will be just fine because I will become your new best friend and just enjoy our new time together forever.

Do My Vote Count

Show me you want my vote. Come to the hood without wanting to throw up. Show me my vote count when times are tough for us, will you show up for us? Because every year, we know nothing about you until it's time to elect you for something. All we want is to be a part of something because all yall do is make us feel like we are nothing. Because I don't see your face around here, sharing tears with us and having fears of what today will bring to us. Will it bring joy or pain? We don't know and that's what drives some of us insane, while the rest try our best to maintain. Show us we really matter. Do you even know my name? Are you really going to make a change for the good for us and not just give us a beautiful speech? Will you teach us about wealth so that we won't stay poor? Will you bring greatness to our front door in the darkest part of town? Because I've never seen you around but you want my vote. Asking me if I'm down to give u my vote, are u going to give me hope for a better tomorrow because today ain't looking good at all so, I'ma ask you one more time, do my vote count?

Juneteenth

No more will I ask "Master, can I go to the restroom?" Master there is no more room for me. Master, can I have something to eat? Master, where can I sleep? Master, are you ok? Master, can I pray? Master, I'm not feeling well, do I have to go to work today? Master, can you find me a pastor for my wedding day? Master, I'm doing good today. Master, this is my son Jr, can he go outside and play? Master, she is my 1st cousin, don't make me have sex with her no more please. Master, don't make me bleed. Master I'm sorry, I'll get on my knees. Master, I'm sorry for being mean. Master, forgive me please. Master, no sir I can't write or read. Master, yes sir I'm a hard worker. Master, don't hurt her please. Master, why can't I go to church with y'all? Master, why do you love to see me cry? Master, you say you love me but you really hate me but you don't want to see me die. Master, today is my daughter's birthday, can she have some cake? Master, I need to clean up, can I use your lake? I really hate that my ancestors went through this for us and I wrote this poem just for y'all and I love you all.

The Killer from Hell

All she wanted to do is kill somebody or go to jail. She didn't care about anything but herself. She lost the battle with love when she was only ten because her grandad kept messing with her over and over again and when she was 21 she found out her grandad is her real dad after her mom passed away. Now you can see the hurt and hate on her face. She became a call girl on a website and looked for old sugar daddies night after night and killed each one after she took their love away. Then she made sure they couldn't breathe life another day because of her granddaddy and he became a pastor with a fake smile.

When the rain and sun is out at the same time you can catch him beating on his wife because he thought it was fun and wild. Her brother became a police detective after the killing of old men got out of control in his home town all because he didn't want his grandpa to be next. He loved his grandad so much without knowing all these killings were happening because of his grandfather's touch.

In the brother's eyes his grandpa could do no wrong but in her eyes, everything he did was so wrong. On one cold Wednesday night, the pastor was having bible study and just laughing with his people without knowing the killer was in the room. She changed her look, shaved her head bald, put a nice wig on, changed her face with make-up and contacts and changed the way she walked and talked. The pastor kept asking her, "Do I know you?" She said "Maybe you do or is it just deja vu?" The brother was in the same room, he thought what she said was kind of crazy and he remembered doing his research and finding out that the killer was a female so he yelled "Put your hands up!" with his gun pointed at her without knowing it was his sister.

The pastor started yelling at the brother "What the hell do you think you're doing with that in the Lords' house?" While the brother is distracted by the pastor, the killer gets away. Now the brother thinks he knows who the killer is because he saw the killer's face. Years of smart planning, the sister finally figures out how to get to her grandad. She follows him to a weird looking building.

The brother was following her for years dong some smart tracking and he followed her to the same building she thought she trap the pastor to only find out later he was trapping her she pulled out a gun and pointed it at the the pastor while his back was turnt and she had a mask on and dress in all black smelling like death while the pastor was dressed in a all white suite. She told him to say his last words before she took his last breath away.

    The brother came behind her and yelled "Freeze! Drop your gun and put your hands up and turn around" while he had his gun pointed at her and she did it, then he said " I must see your face, before I take you in ". The pastor said "Kill her". The brother takes her mask off, seeing it was his sister he was so shocked, he couldn't believe it at all. He couldn't kill her because that's his sister. The pastor had a shotgun and came behind her and blew her brains out and the brother asked "Why you do that?" The pastor replied, "She ain't gonna kill me. Why didn't you do what I asked you to do?".

    Before the brother could answer, he stabbed him two times in the heart after he asked the brother to give him a hug and the pastor had a happy evil smile on his face afterwards because he was the killer from hell because he was too wild and the whole time he was a pastor, he got his word from the devil and not God. He did whatever the devil told him to do without second guessing it and that's how he knew to go to the weird building all because he was the killer sent from hell.

We Were Made 4 Each Other

You are a woman and I'm a man, we are made for each other. Our eyes look at each other, our hands feel each other, our lips touch each other, our hearts are on the same beat, our legs and feet walk together and when we make love, it feels like we are changing the weather. When it comes to love, we are like twins. When I see you happy, I'm glad. When you are good, I'm great. When you hate, I become a lover like no other. When you are down, I'm lower than you so I can lift you up. When you are high, I'm higher so we can fly together. Whenever, no matter what comes our way because we are made for each other each and every day. Together we can grow a family with sisters and brothers and teach them how to love all colors like we do when we see a rainbow. God showed me that we were made for each other.

UR

Stronger than you Imagine.
You are tall and not small when it comes to standing up for your light.
You are a child of God and not the Devil.
You are the one who was made for the path you were put on.
You are a mom, dad, sister, and brother, you are a friend.
You are more than you believe you are.
A person, you are a human being.
You are a star, so let your light shine bright so you can see a path through the darkness because you are who you are supposed to be.
So be all that you can be so you can set your greatness free.

No Cap

If you are black you get shot in the back if you run and if you are white you will get a happy meal. If you kill like it's hunting season and you have the perfect skills, I really don't know what the hell is going on. They think because our skin is way darker that we are dead wrong, literally think we are wrong and we deserve to die even though this is America, land of the free. So tell me where is the free shit for people of color? For the ones who don't wear a red *"Make America Great"* hat? Can you tell me so I know where I can get my free shit? They can't tell me because they know what I'm saying is real and what they are saying is bullshit. I know the truth hurts but it will set you free "No Cap".

A Father is a King

A father is a boy who grew up and became a man. Who understands the meaning of life because he helped to create one and for that one, he will be the King and protector for his child. He will give his life for the life he helped to create and he will go without so his child can have. He knows he would be less of a man if he didn't do whatever it took to keep his child safe so he takes the blood, sweat, and the tears so his child can have a smile and happiness on his or her face. He works his butt off to have nothing so that his child can have something. He knows his past doesn't mean anything because he wants to build a future for his child. He knows all the pain that can come with it will be worthwhile, so he smiles and keeps pushing strong for his little one. He is so happy he has a part of him in this life to carry on after he is gone and that's what makes him strong and he never feels alone because for his child he will keep a home and food on the table all because a father is a king.

I Want that Kind of Love

Thanks for coming into my life. One day I'm going to make you my wife. I'm so ready to settle down and I want you to be the one to hold me down while I lift you up and be your king until the end. I want that fire kind of love that is sent from Heaven up above and when we make love Heaven will cry out because it will be beautiful inside and out. I want that love that will make you scream and shout and when I look into your eyes I know that is what you are all about. That's why I must make you my Queen and I will be your King. I will make sure your day is great so when you go to bed at night you can sleep great and have amazing dreams. If you are willing to cry for me then, I am willing to die for you. That's the *"God's Honest Truth"*. If you do a little for me, then I'll do a lot for you until my hands turn black and blue. If you show me your old self, I'll show you the new me because it's who you helped me to be. If you were down I would lift you up from the ground. I want to kiss you from head to toe while we watch our love grow into another level and even the Devil will want us to stay together. I want to love you forever and a day. I want you to be my lover and have my baby because that's the kind of love I want. Do you? If you do, then say YES, so I can be Blessed and say I DO!

Your Birthday

It is the day when you came into this world. Pink or Blue. Boy or Girl. You were something new to this world. You made your mom and dad a better person when you came into this world. Before you came, they were going down the wrong path and you made them stronger to go down the right path. You made them become better people because of your birth. They may never tell you how hard they had it before you came and made it better. You are their world. Pink or Blue. You are their Baby Boy or Baby Girl. Happy Birthday to you and many more. You are the one they adore, the one they will die for if they had to. If they ever lie to you, it is to protect you. Tough love is what they give to you so that you can live strong and better in their heart. If loving you is wrong then they don't want to be right. Happy Birthday to you from your MOM, DAD, FAMILY, & FRIENDS. From Heaven to Earth, no matter what day your birthday falls on, may you have a blessed and great day on your God given Day aka your BIRTHDAY.

Where is the Hope?

I'll close my eyes and paint y'all a picture. Why do they think we deserve to die because our skin color is darker than theirs. I don't understand what's really going on. My momma taught me to love and to make love strong but how can you love people when they think just because the color of your skin that you're dead wrong and you deserve to die. They beat us in the streets with badges, the color of blue. Now we have a president, #45, that hates us the exact same. He says "Make America Great Again" but what does that mean? All I know is that I'm going insane. I have to pay attention to myself so I don't lose myself. So I can be the voice for the people and help the ones who need help so we all can be equal. I don't get high. I don't drink, but I know I gotta do something because time is flying by so damn fast. Now I open my eyes and I talk to you. Does our lives matter or doesn't it or do all lives matter but the ones that are darker. I'm just saying for the people of color, where is the hope?

When A Cop Comes to Kill

Ain't nothing you can do because when they have their minds made up, all they want you to do is shut up and die so they can enjoy their kill. They are killing us for no reason, other than a thrill. They hunt us down like it's hunting season, 365 on Blacks. They don't want us to live or survive. Just waiting for a Karen to call so they can answer the call but not one of them wants to take the fall. They treat us less than dog shit. What did we do to deserve this? Are people of color on yall's hit list? If so, that's bullshit. All we are trying to do is live and survive while living in hell on Earth, all because y'all don't want to let us have a piece of Heaven on Earth and it is so sad that y'all think every black man looks the same when it comes to crime. Why is that? Do our rights even matter to yall? Better yet do Black Lives even matter to you because yall are attacking our women and children now and that must stop. So what's y'alls deal with us that makes yall so quick and happy to kill us?

I Remember U, Paul

I remember you from just the time when you first learned how to wrestle man. How I miss that. The wrestling team is doing super great. I remember when you were dating Candice. I remember when a lot of people picked on you and you didn't let that get to you. While at home you had to be the man of the house for your mom, little brother, and sisters. I remember when the best wrestler in school and the state of Georgia, Hunter G, took you under his wing. Took care of you like a little big brother. I remember the first year of wrestling you sucked bad, but the following year, you didn't quit and you came back and whipped some ass and everybody on the wrestling team fell in love with you. I remember we used to sit at the same table at lunch and hearing you talk, I knew you were very smart. I remember when I got to go to the commerce pool and it felt like my heart dropped and stopped and I never went back. I miss you so much Paul, always and forever I will remember you.

My Friend Jimmy

Tag! You are the man. The Lord looked at your life and said " I got your plan." A lot of people may not understand why the Lord touched you on the shoulder and said "TAG! You're it. Now it's time to come home." While we will miss you so much and your family will wish they can still feel your touch, but they know you are going to heaven and that's the truth. We all know you are going home when you get there. Tell Ms. Rose, we said "Hey" and tell Mac his family misses him and tell Samone we miss him too. God put your brother Frank through a lot of mess so he can have a great message to tell. God put your sister Ca'Quea through an amazing test so she can have an amazing testimony to share. Your other brother and sister, Doin and Tita, are going to do well. Your mom and dad are happy because they know you won't be resting in hell but resting well in Heaven chilling and relaxing and it was so amazing that the love of your life was there with you at the end. One day we will see you again, until then, please keep a watch over us Jimmy my friend.

I Can't Believe It

The pain I feel now, is it real? If so, how do I deal because I don't know how to. Lord please let me know why my eyes are not dry any more, they're filled with water and they flow. You can see my pain deep down inside of them for my friend Fetus. I remember the time we shared on Gordon St. I remember hearing your voice when I went to sleep. I remember how great you were at cooking. I can't believe it, that you are really gone. I still look to see if you are outside and I'm hoping to hear you sing one of your songs. I remember how fresh you and Clint used to be on Sunday and I know I will see you again, one day. I still can't believe I won't get to see you face to face but at least I know you are going to a better place. I remember how good your food tasted. I can't believe you left this place and may you rest in peace and save me a slice of that cake you make in Heaven please.

Everything is Going to Be Well Mr. Blackwell

He was a Blackwell, now he has gone far away from this living Hell aka Earth. He is now in a better place. His kids won't get to see his face but his brothers will take his place and make sure his kids keep a smile on their face. His mom and dad might be sad but they know God said "Job well done!" and sent him to a better place. Past the sky is where he stays. Just know that your family is looking up, waving hey and not goodbye because they know they will see you again Mr. Blackwell and that everything is going to be well.

Chris Got His Wings

It's 11:20pm on a Sunday night. I got the news my friend Chris from high school just took flight now it's going to be a sad night. As I go down memory lane, thinking about the good and great things Chris did while on Earth, he was known to be a big boy with a big heart. He would have given you the shirt off of his back if it was the only one he had. Now he is in Heaven with Paul and Samone. I know he won't be alone. I don't know the pain he endured on Earth but now he suffers no more because Heaven is his home and where he will grow into more because on Earth his job was well done. That's why the Lord called him home on his heavenly phone. No more pain, no more stress. Just him and rain showers of his blessings. I will miss you Chris but I want to tell you, JOB WELL DONE, my friend if you can hear me in Heaven while you're having fun.

Let's Be Thankful

I'm thankful for my mom, dad, sisters, and brothers.
I'm thankful for my eyes opening this morning after I closed them late last night.
I'm thankful for knowing love and how to stand up and fight for what's right.
I'm thankful for my lesson of pain.
I'm thankful for my mom giving me my name.
I'm so thankful for the truth .
I'm so thankful for you and me.
I'm so thankful for being alive and not dead.
I'm so thankful for the old heads.
I'm so thankful for the people with one leg because they showed me that you got to keep it moving no matter what.
I'm so thankful for the people who cuss and not the ones who fuss because the people who cuss don't give a damn what people think about them while the ones who fuss do care what people think about them.
I'm so thankful for having food on the table.
I'm so thankful for tv without cable because it showed me great family time.
I'm so thankful for Rosa Parks because she made a way for people with my color of skin to live free.
I'm so thankful for Martin Luther King because he showed us it is important to have a dream and to speak it.
I'm so thankful for Barack Obama saying "Yes We Can!" because he showed us that we can.
I'm so thankful for Tyler Perry because he showed me it's ok to make your own table and not just have a seat at their table.
I'm thankful for James Brown for letting the world know it's ok to be BLACK and PROUD and to say it LOUD.
I'm thankful for my real dad and bonus dad because without them I wouldn't be the man I am today.
I'm thankful for real love and not fake love because it showed me how beautiful life can be if you can see it.

Person in the Mirror

If you don't believe in me, who else will? I know we've been through a lot together, all I want for you is better. I know we fuss a lot, I don't mean nothing by it I swear. Look at me as I look at you. Tell me if I'm lying or telling you the truth. You are a reflection of me as I'm of you. I just want to know why you are always copying everything I do? Why is that, please tell me. So it's like that? So you ain't going to say anything? So it's like talking to myself since you ain't saying anything. The only person that can beat me is you and I'll be damned if I let that come true. I see you every morning after I wake up and go to brush my teeth and when my phone goes to the black screen, I see you looking back at me. Sometimes you are mean to me, why is that? Is it because of me? If so, tell me. Let me know what I did wrong because we both are grown. I love you and I hope you love me back. I'm talking to you, the person in the mirror.

Crazy Thinking

    Like James, I want to know where Rick is. Ask Brown if Chris is ready yet. Tell Jamie to ask Foxx where the girls are at. Can you tell Chris to stop throwing rocks before I get Curtis to go get his big brother Jackson because he got the strap. I'ma tell Luda I think Chris is crazy because he is so damn rude, talking about move bitch get out the way. I remember the time I was in D.C. I met this young guy who was always wilding out because he thought he was so fly.

    My boy Chico is always eating some kind of beans and passing gas because he thought it was funny. Tell Robert to stop acting like a girl, that's why his nickname is Kelly. Please somebody tell "O" do not try to find "J" and go chill over at The Simpsons House and somebody please tell Kanye he has to leave this place he can go anywhere but west. Please let him know, can someone tell Ben to let Affleck know that he is not a dare devil so he can stop trying.

    Matt and Damon are always together like they are trying to find a Bourne Identity. Let Eddie know that Murphy just got locked up and might get life for shooting an old lady in the toe on one cold night in Harlem. Can you call Will and tell him to let Smith know he just got his Independence Day. Can someone tell Martin to leave Lawrence alone for good sake because they got a Thin Line Between Love and Hate for each other.

    Hey Tyler can you and Perry tell Madea to come back, she will listen to y'all only. Everytime when I go around the block I see Michael, B, and Jordan always on the corner or on the phone but one of them is snitching and wearing a Wire because you can see it from the back of his shirt. That might be the reason his character got killed. Tell Mike to tell Jones to stop saying " Who" because I know back then they didn't want him but now that he is hot, and they are all on him. Donald can you tell Trump that he can't stay no more and that he needs to quit acting like a dumb female dog and just go.

    Mike can you tell Pence the same thing and don't try to change up his game plan and to take the flies with him please because we are tired of your bullshit. Kenny, can you tell Burns to keep giving us that Free Game so we won't become lame. Martin, can you tell King up there in Heaven where y'all stay, that I said "Thank you for becoming a King with a dream for us so our life won't become a nightmare." Joe, can you tell Biden we need him to keep his word for us and don't let us down. Deon, can you tell Taylor to keep making those life changing for the better movies please. What was I thinking, can this really happen or is it just some of my crazy thinking?

Don't Waste Your Tears

Don't cry for someone who would kill your smile because they don't respect you and they are so wild but find someone who will keep your smile up and shining so bright that it will shine at night instead and help you to become the best you that you can be because they are your better half. Leave your beauty killers alone because their job is to kill everything good about you so you will feel worthless and ready to die all because they make you feel like you ain't got nothing to live for find you someone who would keep your beauty and joy alive so that you can see the beauty in the world with your own eyes so you can truly have love on your mind and something to live for and won't be afraid to die after you truly lived your life because they showed you your worth and now you know that you aren't worthless so please don't waste no more of your tears.

I Got A Love & Hate Relationship With My Job

She loves when I go in but hates when I get off. She wants me to stay longer but I must admit she makes sure I keep a roof over my head for me and my kids so that's why I come back to her almost seven days a week. Sometimes she gets on my last damn nerve but I need her like she needs me. I've been with her for years, sometimes I wish I wasn't here with her but I will never let her know that. She gets so jealous when she hears about me being around people like her because she knows that I'm going to leave her so she tries her best to make sure I stay here in one place with her. So, I see her face on a daily, she always calling me when I'm away from her saying she miss me and that she is lonely and sometimes she acts so phony she be asking me do I love her and I be lying my ass off saying yes I do most of the time she ask me why I don't like spending more time with her I said because it feel like you are always trying to take my life away from me. I remember yesterday you didn't want me to say you made sure I left early then she ask me today why I didn't choose to stay she love labeling me as the bad guy when I don't do what she say she always don't want me to take a break but when her friends come around to visit she tell them she make sure I get a break always and that's a damn lie and that's why I got a love hate relationship with my job.

Don't Let Your

Don't let your age determine what you can do.
Don't let your family determine who you can be.
Don't let your friends tell you who you should be.
Don't let your money take control of you.
Don't let your life keep you from your truth.
Don't let your fear get to you.
Don't let the love of your life go just because you want to be a hoe.
Don't let your mind drive you insane.
Don't let your girlfriend/boyfriend make you feel lame like you are less of a human being because you are with them.
Don't let your parents dictate who you should love.
Don't let your heart be cold and not warm.
Don't let your food choices do you harm.
Don't let your job do you wrong.
Don't let your haters make you feel less strong.
Don't let your dreams go to waste all because you want to be lazy in one place.
Don't let your mind wander without a destination to a great place.
Don't let your tears fall for too long.
Don't let the device you hold in your hand control your life.
Don't let a bad cop be mean to you and try to take your life.
Don't let your emotions cloud your judgement because everything you do for your greatness depends on yourself so you must know self love, self discipline, and self determination to better yourself.

I Don't Get It

Can you tell me why everybody hates Chris but loves Raymond? Why is it that the letter "P" is silent in the word phone and why is the word live and live are spelled the same but don't mean the same thing? Why is it that the food that is good for poor people is so damn high and the bad food for poor people is so easy and cheap to get? Do they want us to be weak and die? Why is it that a white man can do the exact same crime as a black man and get less time or no time for his crime? Why is rice and sugar white instead of their true color? Why is it that they didn't want you to read or write back in the days if you were black and not white? I just don't get it at all. Why Did they take all the good skills that help you get a great working job out of high school and why did they get rid of cursive reading and writing in schools? Why do they think people of color are dumb and white people are smart when they didn't give people of color a fighting chance to be or get smart back in the days? Why back in the days until now when you think of a hero you think of a white man and never a black man. Please help me understand because I don't get it.

Time is Up

The white man doesn't know anything about peace to save his life. The blackman knows all about peace until everything go left, then he gots to make it right so he stand up and fight for his rights everyday and every night until it gets right while then white man want to keep everything white while saying make america great again while wearing a red hat because he hate the color of my skin while the blackman was taught to forgive the whiteman while the whiteman keep over and over again trying to hurt and destroy the blackman for no reason the blackman is a hard worker while the white man is a true taker the white man knows the black man got the skills to pay the bills while the white man got the skills to kill not animals but humans and take their rights after they made the laws for the black man to follow and the black man almost follow them laws to a "T" while the white man saying we are all equal but they don't follow the laws at all but they say they do enough is enough the time is up.

The Black Kings

The Black Man does work.
The Black Man does raise families.
The Black Man does hurt.
The Black Man can be monogamous.
The Black Man is successful.
The Black Man is strong and powerful.
The Black Man is strong and powerful.
I had to say it twice because it sounds so damn nice to the ear.
The Black Man helps to build America.
The Black Man is the true definition of a miracle.
The Black Man can be strong and weak at times.
The Black Man got rhythm something that yall call rhyme.
The Black Man fears nothing but fear for something and that something is the people who he loves.
The Black Man is not a thug.
The Black Man shows a lot of love.
The Black Man knows hate.
The Black Man kinda loves and hates his state.
The Black Man is one of a kind.
The Black Man will give you the shirt off of his back plus his last dime.
The Black Man hates wasting time.
The Black Man tries his best not to lose his mind because the Black Man knows he is king and that's why I wrote this and called it " The Black Kings."

From A Street King 2 A Street Fein

Years after years Money Man Mike ruled the streets. He sold so much dope and took so many kids' hopes away because their mom and dad were buying dope from Money Man Mike. Everyday Money Man Mike made millions in the street, not giving a damn about anybody feelings and always killing any competition that came his way he never ever had a wife because he loved the street life too much and he never thought he could get touched until one hot and foggy night he got hit 15 times with bullets from a friend who was trying to take him to his end but he lived through it but he could never walk again he was always in pain he had his shooter killed and his family too.

He started to use his own drugs to get away from the pain he felt inside as he would get high on a daily he was slowly losing everything because of his pain he eventually lost his mind, dope, money, and hope for life and when he did lose it all he could never get it back or right. Money Man Mike was down to his low rolling around town in his chair looking like a nightmare while looking for dope. He didn't give a damn about nothing but getting high and finding his next hit and that's how Money Man Mike became a street fein from a street king.

My Pops

Pop One and Pop Two! Y'all showed me who I am and what I'm supposed to do. One of you is my biological dad and the other one is my bonus dad. I got my trades from one and the other one showed me how to get paid. Without them I wouldn't be the man I am today. I look just like one and act like the other one. One made me and the other helped mold me. But they both played a part in who I am and I am so grateful for them both. I loved them the same because they never went ghost when it was time to be a part of my life. One made sure things were alright for me and the other one made sure I was ok. One made me tough for the day and the other one made sure I got a good night's rest at the end of the day and that's why I got so much love for my pops.

The Plugs Daughter

  She looks so innocent and sweet but make sure you watch her closely because she knows some killer techniques that will make you become a ghost. Her mom is the queen of the county so if you break her heart there will be a bounty with your name on it. She is bi-sexual, she goes both ways. She doesn't worry about getting money because she been getting paid. She loves to get laid and to chill in the shade. She doesn't play any games and she hates lames. She stays in her own lane and she doesn't worry about a damn thing.

  She is ready to be the queen of the county. She knows all of the major players and most of them really hate her but they will never ever tell her to her face. She loves shooting guns for fun and driving fast cars like it's a sport. She hates wearing a purse because she thinks it makes her look like a nurse. She doesn't have any brothers or sisters and she is fine with that because she really hates sharing and she can't stand a female that acts like *"a Karen"*. She is well known in her city because she is The Plugs Daughter.

He Was Ready

He was young but now he is old. He was hot and now he is cold. He was the King, now he is lost without a dream. He was the man, now he is living off of somebody else's land. He was a boss, but now he is lost. He was cool, now he is a fool. He was happy, now he is mean. He was a hard working man, now he is a drug using machine. He was a worker, now he is a taker. He was ready for love, now he hates the word. He was always on time now he done lost his mind. He was one of a kind now he is every kind. He was very kind, now he don't give a fuck about mankind, He was a go getter, now he is a no getter. He was more of a man, now he is less of a man. He was a leader, now he is a follower. He was a stand up guy, now he is a let you down kind of guy and loves to get high but before all of this he was ready.

Fake Love

When you are being real they think you are being rude and mean but when you are being fake they think you are nice and clean. When you are being fake they love every bit of it so they can run all over you but they really hate when you are being real because they can't get over on you and do what they want to do to you all they want from you is fakeness so they can control your greatness. They know if you become real to who you are they know you will control your own greatness and they can't have that at all so they do stuff to get the fakeness up out of you so you can't be real and you can't stay true to who you are. All the love they show you is fake they will never ever show you real love at all. They don't want you to stand tall at all and all they want you to do is keep tripping so you can fall and they will help you up with a fake smile and a lot of laughter because all they know is fake love.

The Love That Made Me

Grandma and grandpa holding hands once again, their love is what made our family tree. They ain't talk to each other in so long but when my grandpa was about to leave Earth and go home, my grandma came in his room so he wouldn't be alone and the love that once made our family tree was floating in the air once again and my grandpa started back fighting to live after he got put on hospice because he got back the love he once was living for. Now he is fighting more to stay here, to make sure my grandma doesn't have any fear and that's the love that made me.

America What Do You See

When you see African Americans do you see violence and when you see white Americans do you see peace and safety? If so, why is that? Is it because you are afraid of darker skin or you hate or maybe because you think having darker skin is a sin to you and white skin is a blessing from God because you think he made white skin in his image if that's the truth you must think black skin is the devil and it is so evil is that why y'all are killing us off so fast I'm trying to figure it out before I say my last words on Earth so please help me to understand put your hate to the side for a minute, let's talk man to man so do you think people with darker skin don't need to live long and people with your skin tone need to live longer if you do think that then you are dead wrong and how can all lives matter to you if you don't think the black one's do. Please tell me the truth while you have your hate pushed to the side. Now I'm asking you the real question: America, what do you see?

Through the Eyes of a Visitor

I see so much hate for the color black and brown. I see why they hate us now and want us to live underground. I see why they love to gun us down. I see why they have a smile on their face when they take the kill shot and we fall to the ground. I see why they laugh like a clown when they see us in pain. I see how they set the rules up to drive us insane so that we can't maintain. I see why they label us as weak and lame because they think we are dumb and we don't know how to do a damn thing and that's a damn shame. I see all of this because I'm looking through the eyes of a visitor.

The Day After

The day after you left I felt alone.
I felt like I was all by myself.
The day after you left I was so sad that you were gone.
The day after you left I thanked God for bringing you home.
The day after you left, your mom and dad were very sad.
The day after you left I was looking through some old pics we took for memories.
The day after you left I knew you were going to be a part of my heart for eternity.
The day after you I saw Heaven open up and I saw you in my eyes.
The day after you left I cried because you were away from me in your place of rest and forever sleep, may you rest in power my dear friend, until I see you again.

The Soulless Man

He was the man before he went to jail and was still the man when he got out, until everything went to hell. He had a girl who he thought was his queen because he was really happy to be her king and when the money got gone she left real quick and his life became a sad song for him and he got real sick if you would see him today you would see that he is very sick all he does now is drink to keep the pain away. You can see it in his face that he doesn't want to see tomorrow so he wastes his day away hoping to fade away to another place because he is tired of his life. In this place he lost everyone he loved so he doesn't believe in love anymore, that's why he hates instead of showing love and wishing he was dead so he can fly away, so he can see the ones he loved because he is all out of love he is a man who lost his soul and that's why he became the soulless man.

Lane My Friend

Lane I know we will see you again. Just hold a place for us, your family and friends. I will remember you until my end. I want to thank you for bringing peace and love to the city of Jefferson and helping my family to see the lights literally when we thought we were going to live in the dark, you became our Noah's Ark. You saved us and helped us to get lights at night by sharing your lights with us at night and I will be forever thankful and grateful for that. I know for your family when they need you they know you are down for them like one flat tire and you tell them to keep pushing if they have to because any trouble in their way it will eventually get fixed and Lane I just want to let you know you will always be in our hearts and on our minds and the memories of you will flow out of our eyes like rain because the pain of you leaving will hurt but we will maintain so we can see you again when we come home. I want to thank you Lane for being my friend.

I See Our Future

When I look into your eyes I see life. When I look at you I see my wife. When people see us together they say that's right because if loving you is wrong, then I don't want to be right. I see forever in your soul. I see me keeping you warm when you are cold. I see our future together as we get old. I see you and me together forever. I see beauty in your eyes. I see my life in you so I don't want to die. I see a love in you that will survive. I see you and me and a child. I see a smile on your face when I get in your way. I see pain on your face when things don't go your way. I see blessings in our way if we just keep our faith. I see love when I look at your face.

Love

What is Love?
Love is something that can be evil.
Love is a blessing from Heaven.
Love is kind and one of a kind.
Love is true and not blind.
Love is here until the end of time.
Love is mine.
Love is fine.
Love is something you find.
Love is better than gold.
Love is cooler than cold.
Love is growing old.
Love is finding your soul.
Love is giving and caring.
Love is knowing right from wrong.
Love is, being strong.
Love is something everybody needs.
Love is a seed that we must plant in us so that it can grow in us so that we can become more.

I Am

I am strong because I've been weak.
I am fearless because I've been afraid.
I am wise because God opened my eyes.
I am real because I've been fake.
I am, love because I've known hate.
I am a child of God because of my faith.
I am better, now you can see it in my actions.
I am more about love now that I know passion.
I am life because I found my soul.
I am blessed because I am growing old.
I am me because that's who God made me to be.
I am tough because I was made to be.
I am free because the truth lives in me.
I am me and proud of who I have become .

This Woman

She is the one that is more the two. When she thought she lost herself is really when she found her wealth. She feels all alone but she knows that God will make her strong. She knows whatever the flesh thinks is right is really wrong. She knows she was a child and now she is grown. She is all about her mission vision and if you ain't about her vision she can't mess with you right now. She is a queen and God is her king so whosoever is about her mission vision is on her team. She knows she must put God first and she will die for him. She knows pain is a must. If she lives with her light then she can't be wrong. She knows that God is king and God is not dead. She knows she isn't better than anybody and she knows the truth hurts but she knows it works and she loves herself. She used to do drugs because she hated herself but now she knows the greatest love ever. She knows love so she can be loved. The woman is this woman.

Cold Nights

No heat in this place but at least we got a roof over our heads. It's hard to sleep at night because people around me hate each other but love to fuss and fight every night. It's the same old thing night after night, now it's starting to get lame and I'm starting to go insane. Why must it be the same thing night after night? something has to change. Or can I be the change at night is when the evil stuff comes out? Do I need to stay inside or out? Do I give into the evil ways, I don't know what to do. I don't have a clue. When I look into the sky at night, the sky is black and not blue on these cold nights. Something must change so it can become something new.

Hot Days

The stress of a day job is tough and very hard when you live paycheck to paycheck and your boss is always riding you and some of your co-workers telling anything but the truth. You work your nine to five just so you can live and survive, then you go home to more stress and you go to your room and fall to your knees and ask God to get this weight of the world up off of your shoulders and chest. All you want to be in life is to be blessed. You have dreams and a vision. All you want is to catch a break but life is too hard and you are fed up. You wonder why life is like this. All you want is for the person who you love to give you a hug and a kiss.

Be You

Be yourself around people. Show people the real you and they will have no choice but to be in your life after you show them your true colors. They can either hate you or love you because it is what it is. Just be you because you are an original and not a copy when people show their true colors let it be and don't try to paint on their true colors. Just be glad you see their real colors instead of the camouflage color they pretend to show just be you and grow.

You Are What You Do

So be careful of what you drink and eat because you will become that. Be careful of what you post on the internet; it can destroy your life, just ask a Karen. Be careful of what you listen to, it can lead you the wrong way. Be careful of what you watch on TV, most of it ain't real. Be careful of what you say around people about what you have because most people are ready to steal. Be careful how you take care of your health because it could lead to your death. Be careful how you treat others because you will get treated that way. Be careful of how you play with others because some people just want to hurt you. Just be careful with your life because you only got one to live so try your best to get it right before you go to bed at night.

My Life Through Music

I got a friend who is a designer. He is crazy as hell and all he wants to wear is stuff with pandas on it. I got another friend. We call him Titty Boy. He is always wearing two chains when you see him all the time. I got one friend who watched the movie Juice and fell in love with it so now he walks around with two pistons and he won't bust 2 shots, not even 1 shot. I got another friend who is big and small. We call him 50 cent because if he gots 2 quarters. He is going to buy him a pie from the store. I had this one friend named James. He thought he was super cool and the ladies loved him and I don't know why he loves licking his lips For some reason.

My friend Keith is always begging and my skinny friend Marvin is always starving. My white friend Slim loves eating M&Ms to death and I got a friend named Luke and he is so nasty. My friend Daddy is name Trick and he love the kids and rapping for them with his sister Trina my friend Lawayne use to go with Trina and he is all about his cash money and his nickname is young money his favorite person to be around with is the person people call The Birdman who is crazy as hell and he act like a baby and the person that live next to me is very short we call him Too Short and he is over the neighborhood watch and he love blowing his whistle at the beautiful ladies and if they act stuck up he will call them a bitch.

This little white kid around town loves popping pills. He is a rich kid who lives in Malibu and this other kid loves riding bikes and getting high. He be talking and acting like a dog sometimes we call him D.M.X the bike kid and my good friend Tip act like a pimp and he always acting so serious that he couldn't take a joke on day he bought a car he act so stuck up with it he wouldn't stop and give nobody a ride even if you was walking in the pouring rain.

God doesn't like ugliness that's why his motor blew in 30 days after he got the car.Tip had a brother he was a real big guy named Phil. I didn't know Phil. He got killed and Tip took it very hard. He kept going in and out of jail and Tip's cousin smoked so much damn weed that his nickname became Dro and he always kept saying he is the best thing smoking. He was very young and stayed Polo down every day.

My mom who everybody call Ms. Patty got tired of me hanging with the Bad Boyz she say they are always getting into some kind of trouble and they won't stop and can't stop and she hated my friend Troy with a passion because he love to fight then act like a Pastor afterwards so she sent me to stay with my uncle reece and cousin blizzle out of state and I meet a cool guy named JJ Evans who love having a good time for the Lord and he told me to be who I am.

His brother Brandon is a cool guy too. My new friends Dee-1 and Pyrexx always keep it 100% in a good way. I love it here. My cousin Tamala keeps telling people to take her to the King. My new friend Trip welcomed me to hang with his crew 1.1.6. My new girlfriend Angie Rose is so beautiful and she is W.O.G= Woman of God and my cousin T. Haddy can really sing well. I went to church here and I love my pastor Mr. AD3. He talked about if you don't have pain you wont know love. My new life here is great and so amazing. I learned how to pray and to be the best me I can be.

Dead

When I was a little kid, I never thought things would get this bad. Them ugly pigs aka bad cops messing with me while I got all these people trying to be my enemy while I'm drinking on this protein shake. How could it be that? I'm a real person, a model and actor. People act like they know me but now my body is cold from my head to my toes all because a ugly pig hated my skin color. Just because I'm a brother. While I'm laying in the hospital bed, I'm thinking about my life and why I don't have a wife and my boys on the block. Then the doctor says I have ten seconds to live from a bullet near my heart. My mom is in the waiting room praying with my dad. My friends post my life status on Facebook. So many people are sad and saying I was a good guy and some are happy and saying I do drugs and love to get wasted. If I did drugs or got wasted, is that a reason for me to die? 5,4,3,2,1 FLAT LINE…… I'm Dead.

More Young Kids

More young kids are dying.
More young kids are crying.
More young kids are not growing old.
More young kids don't know better so how can they do better?
More young kids don't have a childhood because they're acting grown too fast.
More young kids need to learn how to fast.
More young kids get mad and tell you to kiss their ass.
More young kids don't believe in the future and they are the future.
More young kids don't believe in themselves and they are always asking for help.
More young kids have never been out of their town or state.
We must turn this around.
We need more young kids showing more love than hate.
We need more young kids in a place of greatness.
We need more young kids putting in work for a great cost.
We need more young kids growing up and becoming their own boss.
We need more young kids doing better so our future can be better.
We need more young kids knowing right from wrong.
We need more young kids living past the night.
We need more young kids to live so they can have a life.
We need more young kids growing up becoming someone's husband or wife.
We need more young kids chasing after their dreams.
We need more young kids learning a trade so they can get paid.
We need more young kids off of Facebook so they don't get hooked.
We need more young kids doing better, period, but it's up to us the grown folks to teach them better with tough love. That's all they need.

Dark Pass to Bright Future

He was in the land of trouble. He didn't find trouble, he was the trouble. He was going in and out of jail, living in his mom's house raising hell. He loves trying different drugs so he could find a different high. He wakes up mad and goes to sleep mad. He never ever met his dad and he hated his mom boyfriends calling him son and saying they were his step dad. Over time his life got messed up. He hit rock bottom and no one was there for him, not even his mom. But there was this one girl who helped him to get back on his feet. Through her love he found his greater self and she became his wife. They had kids and he made sure their life was going to be ok all because of that one day.

On the Other Side

On the other side is my home.
On the other side is where I belong.
On the other side I won't be alone.
On the other side is where I am strong.
On the other side I can't be wrong.
On the other side is where I will be forever young and not grown.
On the other side is light and not dark.
On the other side I will see Noah who made the ark.
On the other side is where I go when I fly high after I die.
On the other side is where I go if my faith is right with God while I'm on Earth.
On the other side is the new me.
On the other side there will be no tv.
On the other side pain is no more so it won't be a must.
On the other side there are so many colors that come together to see the light in it's raw beauty.
On the other side we love each other and we won't fight.
On the other side is where I would rather have silver than gold.
On the other side is where the weather is not too hot or too cold.
On the other side is where I want to be.
On the other side is where it is just right for me.
On the other side is where I belong every day and night because it's my new home.

The Power of Will

It can make you feel like a " Fresh Prince" but if you use it wrong it can make you become a "Bad Boy" and act like a kid when you are grown. It will make you become the greatest like "Ali" if you use it right. If you are a lady it will make you a bonus mom for the kids who need it. If you are a girl it will make you whip your hair back and forth. If you are a boy it will make you fight great like " The Karate Kid". If you are a man it will let you have your own "Independence Day". For the people who think you are weak with it, then it will make you "Set it Off" with it. The power of will is no joke so don't play with it because it is so strong.

She was Strong

Once upon a time she was strong. Everything was going good for her and she had it going on. One day something happened like a switch from day to night. She began to give up on life. She did not even want to fight to keep her life right. She began to turn up every night, losing sight of what was important in life. She would vent on the book and hang with the wrong people in life. She would say "Turn down for what!" when she needs to get her life in order. She needs to turn down to be a better mom or wife.

Turn down and get to know herself and kill the old her so she can become the new her. Her ex treated her so bad by beating on her and making her become sad. He controlled her life and she knew that wasn't right. Now she talks down about all the good men out in the world. She hasn't realized that not all men are like her ex but if she doesn't open up her mind all men that she is in a relationship with will become her ex. She must realize that she was hurt, she was abused, and she was done wrong. She can turn this all around because once upon a time she was strong.

Jealousy & Misery

They live for each other. They love each other, they don't hate each other. What they do hate is love but what they hate the most is love coming together. They hate having a good time, they would rather you take a gun and point it at your head and blow your mind out instead of being happy. Jealousy and misery don't know how to love, that's why they always hate and you can't teach them how to love because all they know is hate. They do smile but it's upside down, it's called a frown. They love to make fun of a serious situation just like a clown. They are always putting the good down and helping the bad up. If the good is talking they will tell them to shut the hell up or boo them but if the bad is talking they will listen up and congratulate them. But if the good does anything they will just always have hate for them, male or female. They love going to jail and jealousy and misery know that they aren't welcome in Heaven so they are ready for hell because they know it will be their new home. Only time will tell when that is, that's why they set back and drink. They do have fears but they don't care when they dream they have nightmares. They hate on everything and everybody else and not themselves. They need help from themselves but they aren't trying to hear that and that's why they will forever be alone because they are jealous and miserable.

Wire 2,9

Killing a kid for no reason because yall want to be king of the corner now a single mom has to try to live for her other kid when a piece of her heart is gone. She wakes up daily with a smile on her face but it is in the wrong place. She stays strong for her child when he is in her sight but at night after she tucks him in and she's all alone, she cries herself to sleep wishing the kid she lost was at home with her. She asks God why he didn't take her instead. Both her baby's dads are not around. One is in jail and the other is in hell. She tries to pretend everything is well but she feels like hell all because she lost a part of herself.

The Badge Gang Members

The boys in blue, I really don't have a clue on what they really do. I know what they are supposed to do, which is protect and serve but I don't see that happening. I do see them serving but it's bullet's and it's at people of color, I do see that happening. The good ones are ok with me if they take a stand against the bad members but I don't see that happening either. I don't know if I ever will see it and why is it ok for the bad ones to kill us for a damn paid vacation please tell me that. I'm talking to the good ones, what did we do to deserve this? Yall act like we threaten your life and that's so sad. Now I'm talking to the bad ones, why do you hate us so much? I must know, can you please let me know please, I need to know.

As Long As

As long as I have you, I will have right now.
As long as I believe in myself, I can see my greatness.
As long as I can stand strong I can fight another day.
As long as I know right from wrong, I can continue to be strong.
As long as I continue to live, I will not die.
As long as I have faith in God, I am more prepared for my wings when I fly.
As long as I don't judge by skin color, I can have love for everybody except the people who hate me because of my color.
As long as I talk less and do more, blessings will continue to show up at my door.
As long as I fear God and see the light I will be alright as I live my life.
As long as I stand tall, God will never let me fall.

The Power of Color

Rosa took a seat so that I could have a seat at the table. Martin walked so I can have my freedom of speech to scream and shout when I use my voice to talk. Malcolm showed me that sometimes you have to put anger in your situation for them to take your situation seriously. Obama made me see that I can be a strong and powerful man only if I believe it and say yes I can. Taylor made it possible for me to open my eyes and look at television and see me. Blackwall made me realize that I can be rich as I want to be and not poor as they want me to be. E.T. taught me to be the master of my mind and body so that I can control it. C.T. showed me how to use my mind and body to get fit. Dave showed me if you don't be a sell-out then you can sell-out your greatness anywhere. Nelson showed me that you can fall down to your lowest and get back up and be greater than you were yesterday. Keenan showed me that you can literally put your whole family on plus more on to greatness if you wanted to. Curtis showed me that you can have 50 cents to your name and come from a unit from the hood and still rise up to fame and do some good. Mayweather made me realize that you don't have to have a good education to be very successful. Tip made me realize school is a white man's game and it is run very well and we must do better so we can get out of the hood and these can goods. Jordan made me realize that it is a time to make people laugh and it is a time to be serious and not make people laugh because we don't need our past as our future. Ali showed me that to be the greatest you must fight for it no matter what. Dre showed me that you don't have to be a doctor to be very rich. Kelly showed me black is beautiful if you embrace it and that our destiny started when we were a child. Tubman showed me how to be bold and super strong so that I can be my own superhero and that's why I love my color because black is strong and beautiful.

My Mom

A, B, C ... 1,2,3 ... you had me on June 4, 1985.

Dear Mama,
I want to thank you for giving me life and making me feel so alive because without you I couldn't survive. Now that I got you, everything is just fine. I want to thank you for giving me your time and for being a strong single mother on your grind and making sure your kids are straight. You ignored all the hate that came your way and only focused on making sure your kids had a plate in front of them, even if that meant you went without. You worked so hard to keep clothes on our backs and shoes on our feet. You made sure we didn't go without. You love seeing us happy so I want to thank you for being who you are because without that, I wouldn't be here. I want to thank your struggle with us for making you strong for us. I am the man I am today all because you paid and paved the way for me. You were and still is the best teacher for me since day one. You made me realize that I am the great one and you let me know the only person stopping me is me and not you. You showed me tough love and now I know where my heart is all because you showed me love. I will never be heartless because you are my mom and you are the BEST MOM EVER!

I'm Just Being Honest

Will I cry if you cry?
I don't know.
Will I fight if you fight?
I don't know, I'm just being honest.
But what I do know is if I don't cry when you cry, you will always have a shoulder to cry on.
If I don't fight when you fight, I will always be there for you to be strong and carry on.
I will be strong when you are weak.
I will be your teacher when you need to learn a lesson.
I will always be your greatest friend when you need a blessing and that's the truth because I'm just being honest.

My Last Ride

A Cadillac will be my last ride, until then I will open my eyes and keep them open and never closed so life won't be a surprise to me so I can be who I'm supposed to be until death comes for me. I will learn how to be set apart and set free. I know now to be made new I must learn how to be fresh out of the box so I can be brand new aka the new me because I was that young kid from Jefferson, GA with no vision that grew into a grown man, with the vision that led him to television. When I take my last ride I must be done with my mission. I have to hear God say "Job well done my son, now come on home to where you belong" and I'll be more than happy to take my last ride.

The Hurt I Feel For You

My heart hurts right now.
To get away from the pain I will close my eyes or I will sit down.
I am lost now that you aren't around.
My head used to be held up high, now it's low to the ground.
Now I wonder will I ever get to see you again my friend or will I get lost in my sin because the pain I feel for you is killing me over and over again.
I can't stand it here on Earth without you so what do I do?
I am lost without you.
It is true what they say that you never know what you have until it's gone, now I'm crying at every sad song and wishing you were at home.
Now I'm feeling all alone.
I'm feeling so weak and it's far from strong because you are gone.
The hurt I feel for you is beyond me, all because you are home now and set free.
May you forever rest in peace.

Not Your Job Life

What do you do when you are lost? Who do you turn to? Who is your boss? You are up early in the A.M. just to find out you have to work late into the P.M. Life is hitting you hard, you are living paycheck to paycheck. You eat crap all day and you don't feel well at all so you get a beer, to get loose and your bills are overdue and you don't have a clue on what to do. So you drink your night away and hope tomorrow will be better. Day in and day out nothing has changed and you remain the same because your mindset hasn't changed so you go insane and wonder why your life is the same and it's all because you are stuck in your ways and don't want to change. You need to change your mindset so you can change your life for good.

My Heaven Sent

A digital wave is how I met you and you lived so far away but I know the love you had for me is so true and that's why I really love you. When we met the first time face to face I knew your heart is the place where I want to be for eternity. You made me believe in love at first sight and the love we shared on that very night was so amazing. We had eye to eye contact and kissing and hugging without sex that's how I knew you was my one aka The One and Only. The devil was trying very hard to mess us up with what we had by bringing your ex up and the cops around but the devil didn't know you were my heaven sent to me and he can't destroy that if he wanted to because you are my lover for eternity because you are my heaven sent.

Your Life Was Destroy

Your life was a living hell. You were trapped into a no freedom cell. All you wanted to do was fuss and yell and all you knew was you loved to fuss and fuss to love. You were lost in the street walking around thinking you were tough because you had your heat, but you didn't let people know. At night you had trouble going to sleep. In the streets you act tough as hell but behind closed doors, you're crying like a little baby and asking God why your life is a living hell. Then you hear a super strong voice "Only time will tell" and you are looking around saying who's there, show yourself now!!! Then you pull your gun out and you get ready to shoot, then you hear the strong voice again "Stop, cut on the light now!" and you did it and said "What now?" and the voice said "Look in the mirror." and you did and realized that you were about to destroy your own life so you asked the voice how can you make it right? The voice says " You must get out of the dark and cut on the light so you can see what you are doing to yourself" then you say " Alright" then realize at that point in your life you were almost destroyed.

Let Me Hold Your Hand

I want to hold your hand ten years after I marry you and I'll tell you don't fear because I am here. I want to hold your hand at 60 and say Congratulations!!!! Then we can cheer with wine or beer. I want to hold your hand at 70 and look at you and smile and say this is our year. I want to hold your hand at 80 and say we are still here and still together and our love is forever. I want to hold your hand at 90 and let you know that I really love everything about you from your head to your toes. I want to hold your hand on our deathbed, look at you, kiss you, and hold you and share a tear of joy and say we made it.

Memories

Memories of you sometimes creep out of my eyes and down to my cheeks.
Memories of you sometimes make me feel weak.
Memories of you sometimes can get so deep that I can't sleep.
Memories of you sometimes put me in a hiding place.
Memories of you sometimes can put and take away the smile on my face.
Memories of you sometimes can blow my mind.
Memories of you sometimes can make me get lost in time.
Memories of you will forever be on my mind until the end of my time because I love my memories of you.

The Best Friends Life Line

We are not fools because under pressure we keep it cool. We are free from labels but entertain each other like we have cable. We are going to be best friends until the end. We are so tight it is like we are ken to each other, like we are sisters and brothers. I will forever ride for you and however the situation gets, we are going to stick to this shit. When we are mad at each other, we will find a way to get glad for each other. When we get older and you find your husband or I find my wife, just remember I am a part of your life because life without you wouldn't be right and same goes for me as well. We have been through a lot together and it seems like hell but nothing can hold us back from each other not even jail because we are best friends for life.

For A Fee

They will show and sell you anything just for a fee and just when you think you are free they will put a price on it and say here goes your fee. Just because you thought you were free they will sell you a lie and tell you it's the truth just for a fee. If you save someone's life by doing C.P.R. and you crack their ribs, they will sue just for a fee. When you are alive they will try to sell you stuff for being dead and when you die they will try to wake you up to sell you something for being alive just for a fee. If you really think about it, what's free and what does it mean to you and to me, are we really free? I'm talking to everybody of all colors so can someone please give me the answer please. I'm dying to know before I go. Can anybody let me know please?

You All Are Welcome

I want to welcome you
All the ones who are lost, and the ones who stand tall.
This is for the ones they counted out, and the ones that people always count on.
I want to welcome the weak and I can't forget the strong.
I want to welcome the person that thinks they are right, and I can't forget about the ones that know they are wrong.
I want to welcome the young and the grown.
I want to welcome the believers and non-believers.
I want to welcome the achievers and non-achievers.
I want to welcome the people whose hearts are cold, and I want to welcome the ones with hearts of gold.
I want to welcome the ones who mean mug, and the ones that love to give hugs.
I want to welcome the ones who love to show love, and I want to welcome the people who think they are hard and wanna be thugs.
I want to welcome you big or small, I want to welcome the ones who always will answer your call.
I want to welcome the people in blue, and I want to welcome the people who write and make up the news.
I want to welcome the ones who think black lives matter, and the ones who say all lives matter.
I want to welcome you all, you all are welcomed here, so don't have any fear, just put on your holy gear.
YOU are WELCOME! WELCOME! WELCOME!!!

May 25th

That's my mom's birthday.
Will she age or will she stay the same?
For many years she has maintained her soul as a beautiful black single mom of four.
She always wanted nothing but the best for herself and her kids, but she deserves so much more.
She knows the importance of life and she never takes life for granted.
She encourages her children to strive for the best.
She prepared us to understand: for any positive gain there is the possibility we will have to endure pain.
Sometimes we can't avoid experiencing pain, but we need to be thankful for better days ahead.
She's not afraid to give us "Tough Love" and remind us to stay strong minded in this world of evil.
She teaches us to speak the truth because it will set you free and even though my mom has never been a member of the United States Army, she pushes us to be all that we can be.
She knows if we can only just believe then we can achieve.

MAY 25th

That's my mom's birthday.
No matter if it's five, ten, twenty, or a hundred days away.
It will never change the fact that we are grateful for her and we love her everyday.

MAY 25th

It's more than just another day.
It's a day we want to say we love you mom and we wish you a Happy Birthday!

Think Before You Judge

I'm looking at the sky and my eyes are bloodshot red.
Does that mean I'm high?
No it doesn't.
Think before you begin to judge me because I'm dealing with the pressure of the world.
From these people acting like Satan to the boys and girls hating in the streets.
That's what makes my blood pressure high and why my eyes are bloodshot red.
Females walking down the streets in booty shorts and halter top showing cleavage.
Other girls whispered and said " Oh what a slut!"
Head held high female still walks around in the clothes donated to her because she doesn't have enough funds to buy her own clothes.
She only has dress clothes for church or work, so think about it before you begin to judge.
She was overweight and she lost weight fast.
Does that mean she is on drugs?
Nope, it doesn't.
So think before you judge.
She was tired of the way she looked and felt and she knew that wasn't good.
She took it upon herself to help herself.
What she never told anyone is that she saved enough money to hire a personal trainer and that's when she began to work on herself.

Joy, Pain, & Faith of Tavares

On 01/25/1984, the baby of Linda Mackey and Travis Smith came into this world. As a boy and not as a girl, he was raised up by a strong woman and his daddy was a coward. His mom kept him strong and always moved forward and even though life was hard, his mom made sure everything was ok and told him everything would be alright. He was the older brother and always was tough for his younger brothers and sister. He was the class clown because he would act a fool at school and one day he ended up in jail.

He served his time and learned how to be strong and how to carry on in Y.D.C. His family came to see him and told him to be strong. He learned how to sing while he was locked down and he lost his childhood homie while serving time. After about three years he was released and he looked different. He was more muscular so he decided to finish high school and started doing well for himself.

One day he started to drink and smoke cancer sticks, then he got married and had a kid. He was happy with his wife and then the drama started to come into his life. He started to smoke and drink a little more while his life began to spin out of control. He would start fights with different people within the family. It seemed he had to always have a cup of alcohol when he woke up. He began to get really sick and his skin was on fire.

He was in so much pain and his brother told him he must stop or he would die. His brother helped him get his life back on track and he began to use his gift for the LORD. Now he goes to church and sings for the LORD and his light is shining bright. No one knows but once his light was dim and as dark as night.

A Mother's Love

A mother's love is free.
A mother's love will set you free.
A mother's love is harder than a thug.
A mother's love is greater than hate.
A mother's love can love you in your worst mind state when you are young.
You will hate your mother's love while you are young but the older you get you will love a mother's love because a mother's love is a soldier in the war of hate.
A mother's love can move from state to state.
A mother's love can be your best friend, but don't get it twisted.
A mother's love is always in charge.
A mother's love can bring you more blessings from up above.
Never think you are too hard for a mother's love because a mother's love will pull your card.
When a mother calls you by your full name then you know that's not good at all.
A mother's love can protect you in the hood.
A mother's love is a young girl growing into a woman.
A mother's love is a father when the father is a coward and won't be there for his kids.
A mother's love is a brother or sister when it seems no one cares.
A mother's love is putting her kids' needs before hers.
A mothers love is stronger than a powerlifter.
A mothers love looks better than a bodybuilder.
A mothers love is something you fight for.
A mother's love is the only book that can be judged by its cover.
A mother's love can take the least of anything.
A mothers love can make a homeless a home.
A mother's love is all you need so stop feeling like you are alone.
A mother's love is a place you can call home even if you think you are grown.
A mothers love is right and never wrong.
If you are a child stand to your feet, kiss your mom on the forehead

Tell her you're sorry for being a knucklehead and let her know you love her.

Real is Real

When something is real you don't have to say it's real, you just say what it is. Stop judging and labeling stuff so much. If you go to church, and you say everyone is welcomed but that church is known as a black or white church. I promise you everyone won't feel welcomed. If you call it a church of God, I bet everyone would feel welcomed. They would be more willing to give their lives to the Lord more freely. In life, everything is what it is and the only man that can make that change is the Lord. When you are unhappy with your weight and you say you want to lose fat but you aren't losing fat in your food choices then you wonder why you have fat on your body. I'm going to keep it real with you aka 100. You are what you eat, so if you keep eating fat you are going to become fat. If you eat lean, you are going to become lean. You don't want to be fat, so don't eat fat. It's just that simple "real talk". I just want to keep it real with y'all. If you let go and let God have your problems, you will have less stress and become more blessed. If you feel what I'm saying, SAY YES!!!!

What You Live By You Die By

Billy bought a gun for fun skipping school wanting to be cool. He was a fool for robbing people for their money because he thought it was funny. One day he ran up on the wrong homie and they started fussing at each other. Next thing you know you heard a "Bang!" and Billy was on the ground dead. If you live by the gun, you will die by the gun.

John always carried a knife because he thought it was cool. Whenever he would get into a fight, he would pull out a knife and that wasn't right. One night while sleeping, he had a nightmare and his older brother came to wake him because he was fighting and yelling in his sleep. While he was trying to wake him, John stabbed his brother to death while trying to awake him. He went to jail and was sentenced to life all because of his knife. If you live by the knife you die by the knife.

James loved to drink everyday. From the time he woke up, he had to have his cup. He didn't drink water at all and barely ate anything. Over time he started to get sick. He went to the doctor and the doctor said "If you don't stop drinking you are going to die." James said "OK." and walked away. One night he was drinking and he passed out and never woke up again. If you live by alcohol, you will die by alcohol.

At a young age, Mike wanted to get paid so he did little work here and there. He did that to make his ends meet and he was living paycheck to paycheck. He was tired of never having any money so one day he went to his homies who sold drugs. He told him to put him on and he began to sell drugs and became very rich. He had his homie who put him on working for him and the money began to make him lose control. He became mean to people and never trusted anyone. On a very cold night, the homie that put him on came to rob him for money and drugs. He left Mike laying there dead. If you live by money, you will die by money, so live for the Lord so you can die by the Lord.

Father's Day

Father's Day should be for the man who doesn't have anything, but for his kids he would do whatever it takes to get them something. Father's Day should be for the man who is taking care of someone else's kids because their father didn't care to stand up and be a dad. Father's Day should be for the dad that wants to see his kids so badly but his baby mama is tripping because he's with another woman and not with her lying to her child saying he's a bad guy when he's really not. Father's Day should be for the moms who play the fathers role because the daddy is a coward and refused to help raise his kids. Father's Day should be for the man who always pushes his kids to do better in life and encourages his children to dream big and wake up to success. Father's Day should be all about love so I want to take this time out and say I love you dad! Reggie Howard aka Redman and Happy Father's Day to all the fathers.

Conversation With Mr. Banks

Mr. Banks, I wish you were here.
Mr. Banks, I always wonder what life would be like if you were still here.
Mr. Banks, in my mind it seems like I can hear you saying "Have No Fear"
Mr. Banks, they have this saying down here. They say " The Good Die Young"
Mr. Banks, if that is true then you must be AWESOME because in my opinion you died too young.
Mr. Banks, I know you are probably wondering how my brother is doing because you didn't get to see him before you left this earthly home and went to heaven to be with the LORD.
Mr. Banks I will tell you how he is doing. But
First I want to say your name real loud. SAMONE!!!!
I want you to know that I miss you and I hope you hear me loud and clear in your new home.
Mr. Banks, back to my brother. He did his time and got out, but he started drinking a lot.
He started drinking a lot because y'all were best friends and he didn't have the chance to tell you goodbye when you went to your new home because of his situation.
Mr. Banks, it's 2016 and I am happy to say my brother is doing much better.
Mr. Banks, Lil Mike and D. Lo dad died, but I bet you already knew that because you see him up there.
Mr. Banks, if you see Jesus can you ask him when he is planning on coming back so I can make sure I'm ready. Nevermind that, I will make sure I am ready by trying to live like Christ would want me to live.
Mr. Banks, all your friends and family miss you very much.
Mr. Banks, we all love you very much and we hope you keep watching over us.
Mr. Banks, I want you to know that I think about you a lot. I know you are not with us today, but I can feel your face smiling down on me sometimes.

I'm trying to help people daily by trying to get them to live a healthy lifestyle.

I try to have a conversation with GOD daily about being a better person and making a difference in someone's life and being who he wants me to be.

Mr. Banks, one day I hope to see you again on the other side. Oh, before I forget I have to tell you THANKS, because sometimes when I feel like no one else will listen I can always go to a quiet place and have a great conversation with you Mr. Banks.

She Was Down

She was down on her luck and she believed she always had bad luck. She turned to drugs for love night after night and day after day. One cold night when she felt like no one cared and she was about to give up on life, she met a friend who gave her something so simple. It was a blanket to keep her warm during the coldest of nights. That blanket meant the world to her and she realized that it was a special kind of love. After that night she began to fall on her knees praying to GOD for a better way. She found Jesus Christ and it began to change her life, but she never forgot about that person who showed her love on those cold nights. She would offer to buy them food and make sure they were ok after she was back on the right track. Before she went to bed, she would always fall on her knees saying this short prayer: I know who my LORD is and the Devil you will not beat me again. Amen.

My Future Wife

They tell me that beauty is in the eye of the beholder. Maybe that is why you are so beautiful to me. Thank you for coming into my life because one day you will be my future wife. I will love you mentally, spiritually, and physically to the best of my ability. I will treat you like a queen and I will become your king. I will encourage you to reach for your dreams and protect you from danger. When we make love, I will rock your body. I will fight for your love as if it is karate. I will tell everyone I wrote this for you and I hope you love it because it is true. Most of all, I want you to know I Love You.

Child of God

Old man, just don't understand that God has a plan for him. He's outside where it seems that nobody cares about him but he still continues to do a lot of work for a lot of people and everybody knows all about him. He goes to church on Sunday morning searching for a "Blessing". It seems like all he ever gets out of the service is a "Life Lesson". He's hard headed and doesn't understand that "life lesson" is really his "blessing". He just knows that he is so sick and tired of people in this world. He feels like he doesn't have any family in this small town. He used to live with a girl that everyone calls "crazy" around town, so he decided to turn to the bottle and drink his pain away. Hoping one day he can fly away. He always keeps a smile on his face, but his smile is upside down and his head is pointed at the ground. One night he went to sleep and an angel came to him. The angel said "Wake up! Rise to your feet, it's time to get up and eat." He knew changing his ways would be very, very hard. But he put a smile on his face and thanked God for a fresh and new start. He knew from then on, his journey was going to be super hard. But he knew he could make it because he was a CHILD OF GOD.

Made in the USA
Columbia, SC
26 January 2025